The Joy
Of Me

Cover Design: Stock Art

ODARA PUBLISHING, LLC.
9330 LBJ Freeway STE 900
Dallas, Texas 75243
(214) 971.2436

The Joy of Me

The Joy of being me is the hardest Joy to achieve

The Joy of being happy with who I am

Is a desire that I strive to see

The Joy of seeing my beauty has been a battle of the wills

The Joy of just being me was one

I did not believe that could be

The understanding that I am beauty, love, pain, guilt, pleasure, and more

Is the greatest of all **JOY**

- Michelle Fecteau

<u>Acknowledgements</u>

This book is about who I am and who I wish to become. I hope that it brings a smile to the face of many. I hope that this book open the hearts and minds of everyone that reads it.

I would like to send out special thanks to some people that have encouraged me to write "The Joy of Me." There are many more I would like to acknowledge but I would need to start a second book; so sorry in advance!

Thank you:

- Jennifer: a friend that has stood by me through the ups and downs.
- My children: who inspired me each and every day.
- My family: who have taught me how to love.
- Celeste: who gave me just the right book each and every time.
- Laura: who helped me to realize that a new path is a good thing.
- To my most precious husband; who has encouraged me to find myself, to help others to do the same and learn how to discover my true me.

So let's get started; shall we?

The joy of being **"You"** can now begin! All journeys must start with a first step. It doesn't matter if that step means taking a look at who you are, figuring out who you would like to be or maybe just a simple thanks to the heavens for being who you are each and every day. You must take your first step.

The greatest gift to receive is the joy of being me

One of the best things that I discovered on my journey of being me is that I am one wonderful person. I'm quite blessed to be born me. Although, I don't have many luxuries; I have come to love the simple fact that I am me. I'm uniquely made. I have learned to give myself love on a daily basis. I wake up every day knowing that I am in the company of a great person, ME.

This has not always been my outlook. There have been many times over the years that I would have much rather been someone else. I wanted to be someone who did not struggle, who had no worries or who did better in school. I would find myself watching others around me and wishing for what they had. Suddenly, I woke up and realized I had just as much (perhaps even more) just by being me. I like knowing who I am; no matter what the results. I know the choices I make are ok because I make them for **ME**. The simple joy of being me has become one of the greatest gifts that I have. I cherish each and every day I wake up. I look in the mirror and have the courage to say thanks for being me. I now experience the true joy of being **ME** and all that it means.

Stop reacting to who others think you are and start interacting with the person you truly are

We react on a daily basis to what other people tell us about ourselves and how they think we should behave. It often seems easier to act the way someone else wants us to rather than be true to ourselves.

We must stop reacting to other people opinions and beliefs. It's time to begin the journey of self-discovery. We can begin to discover who we truly are by exploring our own beliefs.

The best way (and often the hardest) way to discover the true you is to make a list of your likes and dislikes about yourself. It is equally important that you observe others around you. Most times you admire a trait that they have and it can be applied in your life. You should never be ashamed of who you are; embrace everything about you. Beauty is developed from the mixture of the good and the bad.

One of my favorite things I did when my children were younger was to have play dates with other parents. We would let the children play while the adults got to have "grown up time." Now, my play dates are with me, myself and I. I enjoy my alone time; for, it's where I grow more aware of who I am.

My Playdate Schedule with Me

- Have a breakfast that I truly love (no calorie counting with this one)
- Meditation for ten minutes to one hour (I meditate better on a full stomach)
- Do an activity that I can enjoy by myself
- Write in my journal…this helps me get a clearer insight about me

Believe in the person who looks back at you in the mirror, not the one that you created to please others

Have you ever taken a good look at the person who looks back at you when you look into the mirror? That person can either be your best friend or your worst enemy. Taking a good hard look at yourself is never really a fun thing to do but it's one that we should do each and every day. You need to be reminded that you are worthy of a great life. All you have to do is reach out and claim it. (Now here comes the fun part, close your eyes and see the life you wish to live and open them and see it in the eyes of the person in the mirror.)

Wow! That wasn't so hard was it? Ok, so maybe it was, but now try to remember what you saw and don't lose that vision. Don't get me wrong here; I don't want you living in a dream world. You still have to face what's going on around you, but I do want you to start believing in the person you see in the mirror and not to let them down.

People cause pain without meaning to. We each order our world to make it easier to deal with and that includes labeling and putting others in neat little boxes. Often those little boxes are cramped; stuffy and just don't fit right. I found myself climbing beyond the walls of my box. It was too cramped! This proved to be very challenging, because my friends and family who built the box kept trying to put me back in it. Yet, the challenge was worth it. I had to get to where their opinions didn't matter. I gained joy by becoming truly me.

Try to look at the person that you truly are when you look into the mirror. They say that the eyes are the window to the soul. It's time for you to look into your own soul and define who that person is. I will say this over and over during the course of this book; this is not easy and it will not always be fun. Yet, it's the greatest of journeys that you will ever take and possibly the hardest.

There are going to be times when you want to stop and just go back to being what everyone's been telling you to be. Is it truly the life that you want to live? Is it what you dream about? Do you see smiling eyes when you look at yourself or do you see a soul that is crying for you to listen? It's ok to cry when you look into the mirror and to laugh as well, one of the best things that you can do is to find an affirmation that speaks to the soul. You must repeat it every day until it becomes true.

Exercise

Create a set of affirmations that reinforce who you want to be or what you want to bring into your life. To create an affirmation there are 3 key things: 1. Write your affirmation in the present tense, as though the change is already a part of your life. 2. Write it in the positive. For example: I am strong and trim, vs. I don't have jiggle arms. The words don't just reinforce what you don't want, jiggle arms, and you'll keep getting what you don't want. 3. Repeat the affirmations for at least 21 days. A new habit should begin to form.

Examples of affirmations

- I am my own authority. (I am not affected by negative opinions or attitudes of others.)
- I count my blessings and rejoice in my growing awareness.
- I believe in the person I see in the mirror therefore I believe in myself
- (Add to Resources section of book in the back: First two affirmations were found at: http://www.ismckenzie.com/17-affirmations-for-building-self-esteem/
- The last was written by Michelle Fecteau.)

Now that you have opened your eyes go to the mirror and see your beauty

Once a person has started with affirmations and the belief that they are deserving of a good life, it's time to see the true beauty that is within. I say my affirmations out on my porch each morning; so that I can see the beauty of the world, as well as myself. Beauty has many definitions and it is never the same for everyone. Many see beauty in nature where others will see it in a shoe store. Society has tried to tell us what is beautiful and what is not. Unfortunately, society always changes over and over again. True beauty is the belief in one's self and loving yourself unconditionally. This will not always be fun or simple to do. Beauty must first and foremost start from within.

I have met many people over the course of my life and I have come to see that the most beautiful person is the one who has fallen in love with themselves. It has nothing to do with whether or not they are a size 3 or 30. It has everything to do with the fact that they love who they are and believe in who they are. My mother is a great example of this. It's not that she's model thin or portrait beautiful. It's because she is one happy within herself. She has a contagious laugh. It is loved by many. This is one of the many reasons that she is so beautiful for she finds happiness in all that is around her even when things are tough. I can count on my mom to make me smile and find beauty.

Exercise

Earlier, I said that when you have a play date with yourself to make sure that you find something that you enjoy doing alone. Some things that can help you to see beauty is to take pictures or to just go for a walk out in nature or in your own neighborhood. Try it!

Your day belongs to you; only you control it

Good morning and welcome to your day! This is one of the fun ways I like to greet myself in the mornings.

So many times we allow others to control our days for us; so, we don't have to make as many decisions. It is not easy to stand up for what you believe in. Although, standing up for yourself can cause others to get upset; it will cause you to be happy. I have had and still have a hard time with this one. Taking back control of what is already mine is not easy. Knowing that something you do may cause some to be hurt or sad will always be hard.

It has never been a goal of mine to hurt people. However; I found myself being unfulfilled when I'm catering to others happiness. I love helping people but I had to find balance. A balance between helping others and living my life. I learned to make my own choices and not allow others to make them for me.

As I said before this is a hard one for me but it has been a wonderful awakening to see that I can be the controller of my day, and still help the people that are a part of my life, except now it is not to the point that they get to decide what it is that I do with that day, that is what I get to decried. Once you start listening to what your heart is telling you, the truth about how you need to go about your day and live your life will be clearer and much more enjoyable.

Exercise

Make a list of the things that you enjoy, then plan a day around these things. You can invite others to join.

Find the joy of knowing that you can make your own choices.

Each day is a new beginning for you to choose to be "YOU"

Making the choice of learning who you are as a person is going to be a life long journey.

One of the greatest gifts is that each and every day we get to start fresh and work towards being better than the day before. "You" can be can be challenging and fun all at the same time.

Any given day can be filled with joy and sorrow. How you chose to be that day will help to decide what kind of day that you have. You're thinking controls you're your day. You can decide that you will have a good day or bad day. You must turn all situations into how you see them.

Have you seen the commercial on TV where the person makes a choice in the morning to have a good breakfast instead of the bad one, and for the rest of the day they make good choices about what they eat and they feel great and enjoy there day. Whereas, the other person has a bad breakfast and makes bad food choices and just runs out of energy at the end of the day, and is not able to truly enjoy the day that they have been given.

Life is a lot like that! We can make the choice to have a good day and be a joyful, understanding, fun with a great outlook. We can be the one that drags every one down with them just because the stumped their toe, or ate the wrong thing for breakfast.

The choice is always up to you! Make it the best by choosing to be happy in who you are and rejoice in that choice.

Exercise

At the end of your day open your journal and write down how you made a choice to have a good day over a bad day. How did it make you feel and the people around you?

Facing your Fears

I want to start with a great big thank you to my wonderful husband; for, helping me make it to the top of Mount Washington. I didn't matter how much I complained, cried or said that I just wanted to give up, he just kept telling me that I could do it. He assured me and that he would be there for me the whole time. I love you Vince!

There have been times that I wanted the easy life. I didn't want to work for things I wanted or needed. However; this is not the reality of life, we do have to work for the things that are important, and learn how to overcome our fears.   First, we must accept ourselves and then by facing the things that we fear the most we become a stronger happier person through the tears and the frustration.

A good example of this would be when my husband took me to climb Mt. Washington. During this climb I found out just how afraid I am of heights and falling, I also found out that I can overcome these fears. Vince chose to take me up the hardest trail to the top of the mountain knowing that I had a stubborn streak and that I would want to keep going back until I conquered the hardest climb. During the climb I cried, became angry and tried to quite a few times as well. My wonderful husband helped me by staying by my side pulling me up holding my hands and giving me words of encouragement the whole time. He never showed anger or frustration, he just kept letting me know that he was there.

It would be worth it in the end. He was so right. On the trails I learned an important lesson. I learned that when I tried to quiet that I was afraid of the outcome, would I do it right would I make someone mad, would I be able to look at myself in the mirror and be proud of what I saw.

I had a long list of why I should not do things, simply because I was afraid of failure, and of just being myself. I have gotten to where I do not have to take the hardest road to learn what I need to know. I know how to face the fears of my life, I can now see that I am able to do all that I want and be happy in the choices that I make.

When Vince helped me to the top of the mountain he helped to start the process of facing the fears of my life. Learning that I was afraid but that I could face that fear and overcome it at my pace, although it may take me a little longer than some people I would be able to conquer whatever fear I had and I would come out the stronger person at the end of the climb.

<u>Exercise</u>

Make a list of the things that you are afraid of and why, then chose one of the items and write out a plan on how you can overcome that fear. It does not have to all in one day but make a plan and follow through with it until that fear is conquered.

The greatest gift that you will receive is when you embrace all that is you are

Take a moment to think about how great it feels to get a really good hug from someone that you think the world of. Learning to embrace all that you are is a wonderful gift and a joy once you wrap your arms around yourself. You will start to see the world in a new light. It's like putting a pair of the glasses for the first time.

Once you embrace the person that you are; keep embracing yourself. You will learn to love yourself as you grow. You will be able to have the world in the palm of our hands.

Exercise

Take a moment to give yourself a hug. Then thank yourself for who you are and who you are becoming and make sure that at the end of the day you are happy with who you were during that day.

The first smile of the day should always come from your heart

This one is for all of us but mainly for all of you wonderful people who need that shower or cup of coffee before anyone can speak to you. Some live right here in my own home. I'm the one that will drive them crazy; for, I wake up most times happy and ready to talk!

Now, is the time to learn to smile from your heart; for, this is the most beautiful smile that you will see, or feel. Stop and watch a child smile and see the joy, and the love that they have.

Learn to smile at yourself. There is no judgment because you are loving you. The one that you will always be able to go to when things get tough, when you are happy or, need a friend. Smile at the person that is to be your best of friend and one that you know without a doubt will never leave. That first smile of love from your heart should always be reserved for the greatest of all of your friends, yourself.

Exercise

Now, go to the mirror and give us a great big heart felt smile. Have that cup of coffee or that shower; love on yourself.

Now is the time to live with the joy of a child and be thankful for the knowledge of age

I have always loved to watch children at play and the love that they have for life. The fact that the little things make them so happy, like a hug from mom or dad, praise for a job well done, or playing on a swing. Why is it that when we become adults that we lose that lust for life, and how to be happy with the small things.

I was in the truck with my husband when I saw a dad with his two boys, one was carrying a box of doughnuts. He looked like he had just won the gold medal because he got to carry this precious treasure for his dad. This made me look at things little different. I learned to see just how wonderful life is when I get to hold the hand of the man that I love, or to sit and talk with my children, or just sit and listen to the wind blow through the trees.

It is so wonderful to see the world as a child and even better when you can then add the wisdom of age. As we get older we lose focus on what can make us truly happy, it is not the big house, or the fancy cars. It's the smiles from those that we love, sitting down for dinner and enjoying a conversation with our love ones.

The nice part is that we also have a practicality of how to balance what is needed and what is desired in our lives. We should never lose sight of the small things in life and learn to enjoy life like children at times. We then can see it from both sides. The side that sees all of the excitement of the new day and the side that knows how get the bills paid on time.

Exercise

Go to the park and play; write down how it made you feel.

Learn to embrace the silence so that the quiet times are not so loud

One of the hardest and scariest things that a person will ever have to do is to face the silence. When it's can you hear you heart speaking to you? The quite time is when we must truly see who we are and what we are doing in our lives. Most of us do not like the picture because it can be blurred.

We have forgotten how to hear our selves think. It is intolerable to hear the silence around us. We are unable to hear what it is that God, the spirit or the higher being is telling us. You must not listen to all the noise around you but the soft voice inside of you. Silence can tell an amazing story.

<u>Exercise</u>

Go to your quiet place where you can be alone. You will not need to be disturbed. There are no phones allowed! Take a journal with you and write down what comes from your heart. In a couple of days go back and read what you wrote. It may just surprise you!

Never say you are sorry for being able to cry from joy

I am one of those people who can cry at a drop of a hat. It can be a sweet commercial, a song or genuine words from another. I just have the ability to connect with things and people in a unique way.

It is an awesome thing to be able to love so deep. Sometimes, I have people telling me they are sorry for making me cry. I quickly tell them that it's nothing that they have done. I am truly expressing my happiness. We should never be ashamed to cry.

Why is crying a bad thing? This is something that I don't understand. Crying cleanse our souls in order for us to see within ourselves. If someone should say or do something that brings a tear to your eye then embrace it. This means you have emotions and feelings.

<u>Exercise</u>

Take time and let yourself feel the emotions that are inside. Write them down in your journal. In a few days go back and review.

Tears that come from the heart are what cleans the soul

Some people have said that crying is a way to purify the heart and soul. It is like taking a shower from the inside out.

It's ok to cry and to let go of what is making us sad, hurt, or even joyful. Tears wash away what is hurting us or it shows just how happy we are. Boys are told that a man never cries. I believe that a true man is able to show his tears and not be ashamed, as is true for a woman.

We should not be ashamed of who we are or how we feel even it makes others mad. We must stay connected with our true feelings and not allow others to intervene.

Exercise

The next time when you notice your tears flowing; don't stop them. You must allow your emotions to come out. This will place you into a better mindset once the release have happened. Sometimes, all that is needed is tear extraction.

Laughing at yourself is healthier than self-criticism

So many times in life we are able to see all that we do wrong and expect everyone around us to see the same. We are so good at criticizing ourselves and seeing all that is wrong that we forget to laugh at the silly things that we do. I have chosen to laugh at myself during times like this. When I look back at some of the things I have done; I can't help but to laugh.

Example:

One of my many jobs over the years was telemarketing. This is a job when you have to really laugh at yourself. You have a basic script that you have to follow in order to make a sell. I had so many people hanging up on me or even telling me to find a new job. I even found myself laughing with the clients because I couldn't get the script correct. This is where you either laugh, get mad or feel sorry for yourself. I chose to laugh! I am now able to laugh at mishaps and not find fault in who I am or what I did. I only laugh and move on in life.

Exercise

Have fun today! If you make a silly mistake; laugh!

The most beautiful of plants may have to go through a little manure before it is in full bloom

If you have ever planted a garden then you know that you have to add fertilizer. It helps the plants grow. Fertilizer is made from manure. (animal poop) You can grow plants without this but they will not be as strong or beautiful.

The same concept applies for us. Sometimes it requires that we walk through life's dirty manure (issues) in order to grow into something strong and beautiful. I am not the best with plants. I love them but I have this bad habit of forgetting to feed and water them. I have had the same trouble with growing myself as well, for when I do not take time to add water or the right food I just do not grow as much as I could. The best part is that you get to look at the beauty that is growing and the wonderful person that has emerged from this fertilized soul. Take pride in the day and in the fact that you are you, even if there is still a little manure that is mixed in, it is a beautiful part of you.

Exercise

Start with a small plant and begin taking care of it and each time that you water, feed, or just talk to this new friend take that same amount of time to feed your heart and soul. It can be through prayer meditation or just some quite time for yourself. Watch how they both grow.

Remember the strongest tree started from the smallest seed

I thought of this saying when I was outside. I was looking at a sapling and a tree that was at least a hundred years old. They were next to each other. The fact that they both came from same kind of seed was so amazing to me.

We also come from a simple seed. We start out so small and dependent. We grow and become like the strong steady tree that has learned to follow the wind. The tree embraces the rain and is thankful for the refreshment that it brings. It absorbs the rays of the sunshine to help feed its leaves that bring the shade to the creatures below. There will be winds and intruders that will try to destroy the tree, but they will not succeed. The tree will continue to grow. I like to think that I am like the tree. There may be calm times and plenty of food; so, that I may grow. Unfortunately, there will be times when strong winds and intruders may try to damage me. (issues & people) Will there be a gardener that will help me or will I have to do it on my own. I will continue to grow. I will be the tallest and strongest tree in the forest. I will be able to say that it is me that has grown, that it is me that has loved, and that it is a joy to be me.

<u>Exercise</u>

Rejoice in being "YOU!"

Through the tragedies of our lives we learn to appreciate the smaller things

A tragedy is not always the big storm that comes rolling through and destroys everything in its path. Tragedies can also come in small doses as well. The good thing about this is that always teaches us a valuable lesson. Some even call it "A blessing in disguise."

It can be very hard to embrace a tragedy; for, it tears our world apart. The rebuilding after one isn't fun or inviting. I still have trouble with this. When I went through my divorce I felt I was left with nothing. I couldn't see the bigger picture. I felt like a failure and I had fear of starting over.

If you are living then you will be faced with many tragedies. Our definition of tragedy is based on what we consider a loss or the thing that we hold dear.

Through all of my so called tragedies; I have found that I can get by without a lot of things. I have found that just having the people I love safe, food, and shelter is a really great gift.

I still find myself overwhelmed but I now know I can make it through. It helps me to talk to my husband, journal or just sit and meditate/ pray.

Exercise

When it all seems to be falling apart stop and say thank you for the small things. They are truly the biggest. You are alive and you get to share the love you have with others.

Does your outer self-reflect your inner self?

Now this is where we get to take a good long look at who we are inside and out. I have found that so many people are really many different people the act one way with certain members of the family, another at work, and still someone else with different friends that they have just so that they can fit in.

We are part chameleon in this regard. Yes, I was one of the best at doing this. I could be the quiet girl in the back of the class or the silly one when I thought that was needed. The perfect wife, mother, the daughter that always did what she was told and the dutiful employee. Man, was I tired at the end of the day trying to be all of those people on the outside. I never had time to look on the inside and see who I really was.

I started this journey of finding me and found that my outside did not match my inside. The person that I was, that I am and that I am becoming was not the one that I was showing to others. I would keep things hidden. I was afraid that I may not be accepted if they found out that I did not believe or think the way they did. I didn't want to offend someone by thinking differently.

When we allow the inner self to start shining through it is a wonderful experience. It is just who we are and no not everyone will like it. It is no longer about pleasing others. Who you are is never wrong; flaws make you the most beautiful.

Exercise

Journal today about how you act around others and in different situations. Is it a match to how you really are?

Remember to stop and breath it will help you through your day

Thinking about just how wonderful the day is or how blessed we are to be in it can be done by remembering to breathe. That nice slow breath where you just fill up your lungs and take in the beauty of the day and the joy of self-awareness.

This is how you can slow down and have a wonderful day. We sometimes forget how important it is to just breathe. Most of us get caught up in the hustle and bustle of the day. This is just how society have trained us. I now try to start my day with some quite time of just breathing. My favorite times of the day has become early morning. It doesn't matter what the weather is like. I just start to breathe. I embrace the beauty and enjoy the scurrying of animals that's in my view. This has become a driving life force for me. This prepares me for the day to come. I have a much better day when I take the time to make this happen. You should try to find a joy in listening to your own breath. It just brings another feeling of knowing that you are alive.

<u>Exercise</u>

Embrace the start of a new day by going outside and breathing. There is nothing else to be done. Only breathe!

Once you learn to fall in love with yourself you can love others even more

This should be the easy part to love yourself. Unfortunately, most people have a hard time mastering it. I have had the hardest time falling in love with myself. I could always tell you the things that I have done wrong or the things I needed to change about myself. I could make it look good for everyone around me. I was really sad and angry; therefore, I could never really love or accept love. I started my love affair with myself; I realized I was worthy of love. It didn't matter what others thought. I encourage you to fall in love with yourself. You must learn to love out loud.

Love will not always feel good. It can truly hurt to love, especially, when we are loving ourselves. We are our hardest critics. The best thing to do is to start that love affair with a wonderful person, "YOU."

<u>Exercise</u>

Write down how you wish for someone to love you and start by loving yourself in that manner. Journal on what you discover.

By stopping and listening to mother earth we can hear what the soul has to say

I'm one of the biggest fans of mother earth. I believe that she has a lot to teach us if stop and listen.

You can listen to mother earth so many ways: sitting outside, listening to the animals, enjoying the nature,etc. One of my best thoughts of this is when Vince and I went hiking and there was a small waterfall. I wanted to stop and sit and meditate for a while and listen to what I needed to hear. My husband Vince can just stand and watch the water and hear with his soul.

It is quite intelligent that souls have great insight. So slow down, listen and enjoy the world that you are in for mother earth is here to help you as is your beautiful soul.

Exercise

Find a place that you feel close to your god and just sit and listen with your heart and soul. Write down what you discover.

Remember to empty out the old so the new can come in

This is when we learn how to do spring cleaning on ourselves. I hate to clean the house, but at the same time I cannot stand a dirty or cluttered home. This has not always been true but the more I clean out myself the more I find that I need my home to be the same way. In order to make room for anything new; the old has to be removed.

The same is true in our lives we have to get rid of the old ways, the ones that just do not work anymore to make room for what is to come. I am not saying that you need to just throw it out but maybe tuck it away in a pretty little box and store it in the attic someplace that way if you need it later it will be there. There will be something's that just have to go, like that old pair of jeans that have holes in them, and they just do not fit anymore they have served their purpose but now it is time for something better.

I have cleared out a lot of things through this journey of finding the joy of being me and I have put some up in the attic to take out later on to see if it is something that I wish to keep, if there needs to be some alterations done, or if it just needs to go. This is a process, not something that is done in a day, but we have to make room for the new. We have to find space in our heart and soul for the changes to come.

It is like the story of the monk that was teaching his pupil. The student asked "Why was he having trouble learning what he was trying to teach him?" The monk began pouring water into a glass until it was overflowing. The student then asked "Why he was trying to fill a glass that was already filled?" The monk just smiled at his young student and said the glass was like him. It was so full that he could not add anything new. Once he poured out some of what was there then there would be room for a fresh cool glass of water. Many times we are the students. We think that we already know all that we need to know to be complete; this will never be true. Life will keep changing around us. We must change with life. We all must take time to do a little spring cleaning and clear out the clutter that may be in our hearts. Get ready for the new and wonderful things that are about to arrive once you find the joy of being you.

<u>Exercise</u>

Make a list of all of the things that you do, hobbies, work, etc. Make a list of what makes you happy. Make another list of the things that make you happiest. Which ones make only others happy? You may be suppressed at which ones are which.

The fear of the unknown paralyzes the soul

This has been a hard one for me. I have been a true example of this. I have become more afraid as I get closer to finishing this book. What if people do not like the book? What if I can't find a publisher? I had too many "what ifs!" All of these questions went through my mind. I was beginning to feel overwhelmed. I began to realize that it's not about me. It is about what my soul has to say. I had to let my words flow as they come in order for my soul not to be paralyzed.

Fear is not a thing of joy but it's one of growth. If you do not face your fear; you will not grow. You will stay stagnate or paralyzed in one place. Facing the things in our lives that are the most frightening for us is the most rewarding. We are able to keep moving upward and on to better things. When I climbed Mt. Washington, I was very scared but now that I have made that climb I have come to realize that I can do anything that I put my mind to. I can finish this book and see what happens.

I still have the fear of the rejection; great joy exists as well. I'm very proud of what I have completed. I have faced great fear and have once more came out on top. I have not paralyzed my soul by putting it in a cage. Now, it's set free. I'm watching it grow into something beautiful and wonderful, me.

Exercise

Pick something that you have a fear of and determine how to face it. Write down in your journal your plan.

From the loudest scream to the smallest whisper; silence speaks the loudest

Many people like to believe that you have to be either really loud, or you have to whisper to get others to pay attention to them. The truth is that when we are silent; people start to take notice and listen to what is being said. The same is for the heart; for, we cannot hear what is being said if we are yelling or busy. Silence is one of the most beautiful sounds that we can hear and one of the greatest places to be able to hear what all is being spoken to us from the soul. We tend to get so busy doing everything that we think that needs to be done that we forget to do what is truly important and listen to the silence. It is in the silence that we face the truth and focus on what is needed and not drowning out the thought of the mind and soul, but to actual hears what it is that they are trying to teach us.

Exercise

Go and sit someplace that is quiet and away from all distractions. Just sit there about 5 minutes and continue up to an hour.

Except the guidance from others but find true wisdom within yourself

There are so many places that we can find guidance today, in books on TV from friends, tapes or even online. These are all wonderful places to reference to. I have had my favorite books, little words of wisdom or advice from friends and family that have helped me to start my journey.

The one thing that they all have in common is that they are guides; they are not rule books on how to live life. You have to start listening to the wisdom that is you to find what is best for you. I have a couple of very close friends that I will go to when I am having a hard time in my life and my husband is one of those. They all have different ways of looking at problems or situations. You are your wisest council because your instincts are normally right.

Exercise

When next you sit to write in your journal take a moment to think about a situation in your life that you want advice on. Write out what you would tell someone else to do in the similar situation and discover just how smart you are.

Don't let you dreams fade into the winds

I have had many dreams over the course of my life and I have given up on many of them. When I did I felt like I failed myself in some way. I have learned that I needed to dream. I needed to hang on to those dreams and let them come to life; not just fade away.

Our dreams are a gift and one of the things that can make us strong. One of my greatest dreams was to write. I never thought that I would be good at it. I was lucky; for, my dream came back around to me. It still appeared in my fears and doubts. I love my dreams, regardless of how others view them. I have a dream of travelling and seeing this most wonderful world that we live in. Will that dream come true? I do not know but I believe in it. I will nurture it on a daily basis with my hope in its existence.

Exercise

What is your dream? Is it to travel, write a book, get married, or start your own business? Whatever it is, believe it and go for it. Do what makes you happy and complete. Your dreams will help you on your journey and bring a smile to your heart. Write down your dreams.

The power of inner strength has the power to conquer all

There have been many conquers over the course of history. Some who did it quietly, some with a big bang, but they all had one thing in common and that is inner strength. They believed that they could do whatever it was that they set out to do. You have the power to be a great conquer as well .It may not be one based off a war but you still can be defined as a hero. Once you find your inner strength you have the power to make your world a better place.

A place that is one that you can take joy living in, that is peaceful, fun, nurturing and fulfilling, Inner strength does not come over night it is a process just like everything else that we have to do. It will take time. For some it will come faster than other. For me it took a while, I first had to love who I was and learn that it was ok to just be me and be happy in being me. Then my inner strength started to grow and my confidence started growing and became like the kudzu in Georgia. It just went like gang busters and had a mind of its own and has not stopped growing. It is a joy each and every day to watch the growth of my inner strength.

There have also been days that I have felt that it died and that I had no more strength left. I will then go back to my quiet place and just sit and listen to the wind and the silence until I heard my soul start to speak to me.

We all have low days. It is okay to have days like that. You just need to remember to love who you are. The key is to believe in who you are and embrace your inner strength.

<u>Exercise</u>

Write yourself a letter praising yourself. Write down all the things you love about yourself and the growth you are witnessing within.

Out of blindness; I gained sight

I want to say "I love you daddy" to start this one off. It was my father who inspired these thoughts.

My dad is one of the most amazing people on the face of this earth. He has always been the provider for our home. He has given is love and taught us right from wrong.

My dad got a fungal sinus infection that caused him to lose his eye sight at the age of 74. Most people would have lost it but not my dad. He was not over joyed by what happened but he did not let it take over his world. He adjusted to the new challenge and remained the same at heart. Although, he may knock over a few more cups then what he use too.

In watching my dad deal with his challenge; I realized that out of the darkest places that we can gain sight. If you close your eyes and look inward then it is a whole new world that you will be able to see. I came to see that in blindness there is sight. There is understanding of what we look at each day but never see.

Look at the world that is yours, not with your eyes but with your heart. You must not rely on what others tell you it is or even what you think that it may be. Only look with your heart.

Thank you daddy for helping me to see. I love you!

Exercise

Think about something that you see every day and write down what it looks like to you. What color it is, how tall, and so on. Go and find that something and see how close you were to what it really looks like. Sometimes it is not the actual object that is beautiful but the memory of it.

Strength sometimes come in small packages

One of the strongest men I know is my father-in-law Paul. Now, he may not be one of the tallest men I know, but he is truly one of the strongest.

I am not speaking of the strength of muscle; although, he is that too. I'm talking about strength of character and heart. This is a man who started his own business to make sure that he could take care of his family. He love to say that he wasn't been perfect but he did his best. He always keep his word to you. He truly believe in his word being his bond. I have learned a lot from this man and take great pride in the fact that I have the joy of being his daughter –in –law. You do not have to be larger than life or the biggest to be the best.

You just need to be yourself.   Strength is not always the bodybuilder that can lift the heaviest weights. Most times it's the little guy that stood up to the bully, the shy person that gave the speech or father that held you when you cried.

Strength is in the love that we show to others and to ourselves. It's not in the big fancy gifts but in hugs and the smiles that are given without the thought of getting something back. Your inner strength may not be large in size but it's a giant when it comes to what it can accomplish. It's very great.

Exercise

Examine what it is that you believe makes a person strong. Describe what is strong about yourself.

Don't live your life in mediocrity; live it to your fullest desire

I use to think that I was living a great life because my bills were paid, and I could go out to each dinner once in a while. My life was not bad but there were so many things I was missing. I wasn't doing any fun things like: hiking, picnics or saving for a vacation. I just getting by and was happy with that. I no longer want to be just happy with just getting by. I want more than just a peace of the pie. I want the whole pie and a scoop of ice cream!

Living to our fullest desire mean that we have to take chances. This is scary because we automatically think we will fail. We take chances to reach for the stars, desire more for ourselves even if that means traveling around the word or just taking a pottery class. No desire is wrong as long as it's yours. Know that your desires are worth having and worth working for. You must never settle for less than what you deserve or see.

I am happy to say that I did not settle for anything less than what I deserved and wanted. I deserved and wanted my husband, Vince. We may not have a big fancy house or fancy cars. We have better; a life together. I would encourage anyone to always go after what fulfills you. You don't need anything that have you still thirsty.

<u>Exercise</u>

Write down what it is that you truly desire and what it will take to make it happen. After a few weeks look back and see what has started to manifesting into reality.

Let your life soar like the owl

Bet you thought I was going to say eagle, well I fooled you, so now I will tell you why the owl verses the eagle.

Although, the eagle is a grand bird and a great hunter and one of the most beautiful in flight, the owl is my passion. The fact that it can see in the dark, fly in silence, and is a symbol of wisdom has made it my favorite of all the winged family that live on this wonderful earth.

Owls are farsighted and see best in low lights.(which also draws me to them for they are like me farsighted) I am also fond of the fact that the owl can see ahead and even better when things are dark. They will use the small feathers on their wings to help catch their prey. Owls are known for being able to fly in silence; so, that they can hear their prey. This enables them to gain what they seek. They are not well known for building nests; for, they will make their home where ever they can find it. If we were more like the owl and would listen to what is in the silence than we too could hear what is waiting for us. It would be easier to embrace who we are. The owl does not try to be like the eagle nor the eagle to be like the owl. They are pleased with who they are and live their life to the fullest. This is a lesson that we should take from them and learn to be happy with who we are. I have learned much from my friend the owl.

Exercise

Make a list of what it is that you wish to have in the future and what it will take to make it happen. Become farsighted like the owl.

Being naked is not the sin; covering the truth is

Now you may be thinking that I am going to be talking about walking around without any clothes on. I do not have any problem with nudity and I understand that it's not for everyone. Nudity is not the topic at hand.

The topic is covering up the truth of who we are. We need to stop trying to dress up all fancy; so, that everyone around will think that we are perfect. In reality, if we have to cover the truth of who we are, how are we going to be able to be become who we are meant to be? Being naked is being able to show yourself in the raw. The good, the bad, the ugly and the beautiful. It's in the nakedness of the soul that we find the truth in who we really are. Do not be ashamed of the person that you are. You should take pride in yourself and lose all of the decorations that so many of us think that we need to be accepted.

It's time to let the world know that you are alive and proud of who you are. Let everyone know that you are wonderfully made I will no longer cover up the beauty that is me. There is only one "ME" and no one else is ever going to be "ME." I love "ME."

Exercise

Repeat this simple phrase "it is good to be because I am me and no one else is ever going to be just like me." GO ME!

The life that is lived with freedom is no longer a chore.

Have you ever woke up and just wanted to go back to bed because just having to go through the day was just way to much work. I know we have all had these kinds of days but when this is the norm it may be time to rethink how you are living your life.

I have had days that I did not want to get out of bed and I have had times in my life that I just did not want to live. I did not like it and it was too scary for me. Once, I let go and just started to live in the moment of the day; life was better. I have learned that the freedom of just being who I am makes life a more joyful place. Instead of covering your head in the morning and staying in bed become alive and ready to see just what is out there. Each day opens a new adventure for you to claim.

Exercise

When you wake up in the morning; embrace what it brings. Learn to be happy in all things.

The greatest of gifts comes in the smallest of packages.

I have always been one to love the small things. In most cases, when you see a small box; normally something wonderful is inside. Just think of the person that is being asked to be married; when their partner pulls out that small little box and the joy that it brings.

One of the greatest of gifts is how we will be remembered. The things you do are the things that others will remember about you when you have passed away.

Although you may forget what all you have done throughout your life; there will be someone who will remember you. It's important to make the choice when you wake up how you wish to be remembered today and always. What is going to be the small gift that you give to others at the end of your day and at the end of this life?

My gift is knowing that I was able to find the joy of just being me. I hope that I have passed that joy on to others. It's not a very big box but it was a gift that was given to me. It has brought me great joy. I hope that as I pass this little gift on to you that you can find the joy of being you.

Exercise

Pass on the gift of you to others around and love the day you are now in.

"ME"

Open your eyes and what do you see?

Do you see the forest or do you see the trees?

Do you see the flower or do you see the garden?

Do you see the crowd or do you see the people?

Do you see the body or do you see the spirit?

And most of all do you see sadness or do you see joy?

Allow me to see what needs to be seen

Allow me to be who I need to be

Allow me to say what should be said

Allow my heart to see my soul

Allow my thoughts to be true, my voice to be strong, and my actions to be sure and my soul to be true

Allow me to be me

I see the rain as it washes away my fears

Each drop a new hope a new beginning

It cleanses my soul as it washes the earth

As the drops fall, sown to the ground, I too am cleansed and renewed

Blessings of the days are all around

A cool breeze on my face and the smell of the air

The beauty of the earth under my feet and birds that songs that travels with the wind

A sky that is blue or gray it matters not

For this is my day and I am thankful for the joy that it has brought

www.ingramcontent.com/pod-product-compliance
Lightning Source LLC
Chambersburg PA
CBHW070500290526
45790CB00003B/1034